THE FRENCH TOUCH

INTRODUCTION

Another book on interior design? My shelves are already filled with them and overflowing. No doubt yours are too . . . Books on modernizing a Tudor cottage or transforming a loft into an apartment; on how to live in a cave; on reviving Sixties style; on covering your bedroom in fabric and your kitchen in wood; on rehabilitating an African hut, converting a Greek fisherman's cottage or restoring a manor house in Brittany; on redesigning everything from the bathroom to the broom closet . . . There is no end to them. Dozens of such books come out every year, each in its own way treating that apparently inexhaustible subject, interior decoration.

"Once more, with feeling," says the song. So here is my contribution, or I should say ours, since it is based on the work of the *Maison & Jardin* team. Rather like a guidebook, it invites you to wander through the landscape of design in town and countryside. To be precise, it invites you into thirty-five apartments and houses in Paris, the Ile de France, the West, the South-West, and the South, where you will find thirty-five different kinds of French design: simple, as in a farm in Normandy rescued by a painter in love with genuine country life; grandiloquent, as in a perfectly proportioned Parisian apartment; sophisticated, as in another apartment where the crimson curtains suggest the sultry, sinister world of Barbey d'Aurevilly but also the gaiety of a box at a Verdi opera; welcoming, as in a former silk farm in Provence transformed into a vacation house; classical, as in a villa near Toulouse decorated in late 19th-century style; engaging, as in the wing of a chateau in the Bordeaux region which has been altered and revitalized by a new generation of owners. Thirty-five places chosen among many to illustrate a certain kind of taste, what Chateaubriand called "the good sense of genius."

A summer house on the banks of the Marne, redolent of the sweetness of France. It belonged to Victor Laloux, architect of the Gare d'Orsay in Paris at the turn of the century; the designer Gérard Franc has preserved its old-fashioned charm.

Let us be modest in our claims, however: this is of course not a comprehensive survey of every possible sort of French style. There are thousands of fine old houses whose architecture and furnishings survive more or less untouched as witnesses of the past – at Barbentane near Avignon, for instance, Montgeoffroy near Tours, Jussy near Bourges – not to mention the great chateaux, more or less well-known, that figure on tourist itineraries and would need a score of books to do them justice. Interesting, magnificent, and French they may be, but this book is not about them: it is concerned with contemporary trends in interior design.

Personality counts now rather than safe traditional styles; originality rather than mere opulence; imagination rather than convention; and comfort rather than display. Even if they sometimes seem to include references to the past, the homes that you will see were designed to be lived in today; and they are full of ideas that can easily be adapted. Above all, they have been chosen for their charm – that seductive quality, as irresistible as it is intangible, independent of time and passing fashions, that blooms in any home, small or large, in the city or the depths of the country, that has been furnished with love.

What is charm? How can we pin it down? Is it due to a well-thought-out plan? a particular color harmony? a poetic atmosphere? a chair that welcomes you, a painting that enchants you, a "find" that fills you with excitement, a bouquet of flowers that offers itself to you? Is it explained by that love of balance, of the *juste milieu*, for which we French are famous? Or is there something in it of frivolity, for which we are equally well-known? Could it be that a certain logical, acerbic Gallic wit underlies the creation of a successful interior? Hard to say. But what does seem certain is that it depends on a whole host of varied details and that it raises domesticity to the level of art. And surely charm is what characterizes a French interior, just as timeless good taste characterizes the classic English house, cheerful comfort the American, aesthetic rigor the Italian, sumptuous austerity the Spanish, and intelligent functionalism the homes of Scandinavia.

Houses resemble their inhabitants. Discreetly or flamboyantly, they express their aspirations and their behavior – one person's dreams of nobility, another's bourgeois common sense, the humor of a third, the grandiose ambition of a fourth. You can learn more about people's manners and customs from their homes than from any number of social and sociological surveys. In France conversation is, if not a substitute for sport, at least a favorite pastime. And the place where family and friends gather – the informal *petit salon* or sitting room, the living room, the *grand salon* or drawing room – is the heart of the house. Here you will find the finest pieces of furniture, the best pictures and *objets d'art*, and the softest carpets; here the owner will hang the newest curtains, place the most fashionable sofas, and give most care to the lighting. It is the room most loved by designers and by the mistress of the house, and its decoration sets the tone for everything else. Next comes the dining room, as you would expect in a country where gastronomy is almost a religion. As much care goes into its arrangement as into the preparation of a cordon bleu meal: with its display of dishes on the walls, its candelabra and silverware, its plates and glasses chosen with exquisite care, the table itself a masterpiece of composition, the room feasts the eye before it feasts the palate. And the bedroom? According to our reputation abroad, this ought to be the most important room of all. The canopied beds, pretty printed fabrics, gauzy muslins and delicate furniture should perfectly convey that mood of sophistication and seduction that is, rightly or wrongly, considered to be so very French. Do they match your ideas? It is for you to say. And you must decide, too, whether these thirty-five houses and apartments chosen from the pages of *Maison & Jardin* conform to your idea of the "French touch." For me, each of these places represents one facet of the beloved land of my childhood. Each room displays the talent of architects, interior designers, craftsmen, colorists and others whose taste is matched only by their perfectionism. Not *all* the available talent, though: once again, let us be modest in our claims. To cover new trends not yet part of the mainstream, and to examine ideas that may form the creative world of tomorrow, would require a second volume. Another book on interior design?

My shelves are overflowing. Yours too, perhaps . . .

1

PARIS: THE DECORATOR'S EYE

They are the ones who set the tone, start new fashions, create color harmonies, invent mixtures of styles, manage space; they who, by their skill, coax out the personality of a house. "They" are interior designers. That is to say technicians, colorists, researchers, artists, poets, psychologists – and more. Without their imagination, our bourgeois apartment in town would look just like that of our great-aunt, and our country house would be merely rural; eternal safe beige would still be our favorite color, 18th-century furniture (genuine or fake) would be the touchstone of good taste, and bedrooms would still be bowers of flowered chintz. These "pros" lay before us a treasure-chest of ideas. They let us share their aesthetic sense and their skill. They encourage us to be bold, but also sensible: together with clever conceits and ingenious tricks, they give us lessons in taste. One teaches us how to hang pictures; another how to group objects into compositions; a third how to use fabrics; a fourth how to arrange happy marriages between unlikely partners. Some give detailed information on sophisticated improvements to a bathroom or how to transform a dressing-room into a kitchen. So when Madeleine Castaing, Jacques Grange, Sabine Imbert, Dominique Menvielle-Bourg and other Parisian interior designers ask us in, we should rush to take up their invitation. It is fitting that they should also usher us into this book.

Favorite books and *objets* in the apartment of the designer
Dominique Menvielle-Bourg (see p. 28).

AUTUMN FIRES

Some designers find inspiration for a decorative scheme in a painting, the pattern of a carpet, or the colors in some exotic fabric brought back from abroad. For others it might be the motif on a plate, or a collection of objects, prints or china. Yet others take their cue from the style of the building or the view from a window. For Michèle Gayraud, who has worked closely with Jacques Grange and is a designer in her own right, the spark was a bunch of autumn leaves picked up in the park at St.-Cloud. Faded green, dark red, and all shades from yellow through to brown give her apartment a golden autumnal glow. There are comfortable large sofas, books within easy reach, well-placed lamps, and eloquent groups of objects; and there is, too, a remarkable spaciousness, as the doors between the rooms stand open. It all feels rather like a formal French garden. Might that, too, have been inspired by an autumn walk?

Skilfully composed still-lifes enliven a chest of drawers and a fireplace. To a mixture of bronzes and Gallé glass vases (*above*) Michèle Gayraud has added two little paintings, treated as if they were *objets d'art. Opposite:* Amusing 19th-century ceramics stand below a painting from Cuzco in Peru, which is hung against the mirror. The objects pick up the main colors used in the apartment.

The dining area (*above*) feels like a box at the opera a hundred years ago. The Russian candelabra and Austrian chairs give this intimate space a Central European flavor. A view of the other end of the same room (*opposite*) is framed by a pair of English wooden urns. Note the careful hanging of the pictures and the extra-wide braid that divides the walls up into panels.

Top: The walls of the entrance hall are treated to look like stone, and the floor is paved with stone from Nancy. *Above:* The library with its oak bookcases can also serve as a dining room. Sylvie Nègre used slipcovers of printed fabric to cheer up the chairs.

To make the grand room used as a bedroom less awesome, Sylvie Nègre introduced a mezzanine big enough to hold bookshelves and a desk (*above*). The stairs leading up to it, designed with a nod to Directoire forms, also have the effect of creating an alcove for the bed.

INFINITE WHITENESS IN A LITTLE ROOM

What is it that in everyday life can be cold, like snow, boring, like milk, empty, like the page of a writer who can't think how to begin? White. What is it in design that unifies an interior, makes it seem more spacious, creates super-simple chic and elegance? White again. The apartment of Dominique Menvielle-Bourg, a designer attached to the Galerie Maison et Jardin, is the perfect proof of this paradoxical fact. In what is basically a single room in Montmartre, all shades of white blend happily together, the wood of the furniture and the natural materials of handmade pottery and basketwork stand out to perfection, and sobriety itself seems warm. What is it in these skilfully arranged spaces that is immediately striking and completely enchanting? White, absolutely.

White well-used in a city apartment – in the slipcover of the sofa, the chalky walls, the carpet which is almost rustic, and the painting by Lionel Godart. All this whiteness is offset by the wood of the antique Provençal chair and the two Chinese endtables. The same game of counterpoint is played in the bathroom (right foreground), where a birdcage is placed against pure white walls.

Right: The living room has a Mediterranean look. The shelving is of stone and wood painted white; and the table with its travertine top and foot separated by a column of altuglass and the white-painted folding stools look as though they had been brought in from a terrace.

Looking through the full length of the apartment from the bedroom to the living room (*left*), the view is like a graphic design, incorporating the eloquent shapes of an almost Oriental-looking gondola prow and of the living room furniture and objects silhouetted against the window. Note how the bedhead is a box, concealing stereo equipment.

The bedroom itself (*opposite*) has a strong Japanese, Zen, feeling, though one isn't quite sure why: is it the bed, placed simply on a rectangular base covered with woven wooden strips; the tester, also of woven wooden strips, suspended overhead on two poles of natural wood; the bamboo chair, that looks like an ideogram; the woodcut-like composition of objects and plant against Oriental-style blinds; or the overall serenity? There is also an ingenious touch of Western elegance: shelves and closets are concealed behind linen drapes.

A WELL-ORDERED WORLD

Personality sometimes derives from the ordering of things. Imagine this apartment without its objects: it would be light, spacious, and no doubt pleasant to live in, but it would be ordinary – just like any of thousands of other Parisian apartments. Introduce masses of books, fin de siècle *paintings and amusing antiques, a few pieces of country furniture, old-fashioned chairs, a piano, a cat, a dog, and the taste of an inveterate hunter among junk shops. The result is a unique environment, with the timeless charm that is the hallmark of the antique dealer and designer Anne Gayet.*

White-painted shelves frame the bedroom door (*right*) and a view through to the living room. On the piano (*above*) is a little grouping of objects that include snuff boxes shaped like cats and a painting by Marie Bashkirtseff.

The summery bedroom suggests a Mediterranean siesta even in the
depths of wintry Paris. The bedcover and drapes are of white linen,
as is the slipcover on the armchair. The mosquito net hung above
the bed gives an unexpected and delicious exotic touch.

In the living room, pale walls, ceiling and woodwork set off the
furniture and objects, whose apparent disorder is carefully studied –
in the foreground, a display of tobacco holders in the form of
wooden shoes, and elsewhere small antiques grouped by themes.

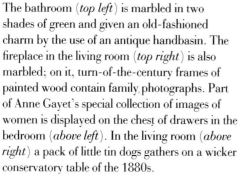

The bathroom (*top left*) is marbled in two shades of green and given an old-fashioned charm by the use of an antique handbasin. The fireplace in the living room (*top right*) is also marbled; on it, turn-of-the-century frames of painted wood contain family photographs. Part of Anne Gayet's special collection of images of women is displayed on the chest of drawers in the bedroom (*above left*). In the living room (*above right*) a pack of little tin dogs gathers on a wicker conservatory table of the 1880s.

Opposite: The dining room feels a bit like the country. The 18th-century Alsatian dresser holds another of Anne Gayet's collections, of pottery jugs made around 1900. The table is covered with a quilt and surrounded by 19th-century bamboo café chairs. As in the other rooms, fine Venetian blinds filter the light and provide privacy from neighbors' eyes.

THE PAST IN THE PRESENT TENSE

Can you make a sentence in the present tense out of statements in the past? Indeed you can. To give it a special eloquence, the owner of this house in Paris called upon the skills of two designers, Vincent Fourcade and François Catroux, who each interpreted her ideas in his own way. Thus it is that an

18th-century interior is the setting for a happy composition of furniture and objects ranging in period from Louis XV through Louis XVI, Directoire, Empire, Charles X and Louis-Philippe to Napoleon III. It is timeless – but also, most importantly, perfectly adapted to the life of today.

Above: The living room. There are Louis XVI candlesticks on a Louis XV table, an English stool serving as a low table, a Charles X clock on the Louis XVI mantelpiece, and comfortable modern sofas. A large Aubusson carpet draws it all together.

Opposite: The dining room, lit by candles in an Empire chandelier and wall sconces, has a painted ceiling that is listed on the register of historic monuments. The embroidered upholstery of the Louis-Philippe chairs is a stitch-for-stitch copy of the original design.

A living room on the upper floor in Proustian mood, with a central circular ottoman topped with the traditional potted palm. Note the marbling and wood-graining on the door.

A 19th-century lantern hangs over the stairs; an antique bathtub from the Marché aux Puces, filled with plants, brightens the landing.

'PLAINE MONCEAU' STYLE

Sabine Marchal belongs to that new generation of Parisian women designers who bring a little extra something to their work – practical common sense? a feminine way of seeing? could one simply call it charm? Charm is certainly the quality she has imparted to the house in the Plaine Monceau district of which the ground floor is occupied by the art gallery of her husband, Didier Imbert: one glance at her transformation of its formal rooms is proof enough. With a few pretty fabrics and carpets in carefully chosen colors, a little furniture and a lot of ideas, she has made a somewhat grandiloquent Second Empire house into a cheerful setting for family life with four children.

In the dining room (*above*) the paneling was stripped to provide a background for drawings by Salvador Dali and silver from Puiforcat. What had been a dressing room became a kitchen (*left*). The painted woodwork was retained, together with the closets, which now hold dishes, but the modern world has been welcomed in – a television, for instance, is set into the counter dividing the room.

Opposite: The main staircase leading up to the private apartments is imposing, but its serious tone is lightened by Italianate games played with *trompe-l'oeil* painting and mirrors.

On a Louis XVI commode, a tablescape of decorative Chinese blue-and-white porcelain picks up colors in the painting and in the swirly Paisley pattern wall covering.

Points to note in the living room, that looks out over the Parc Monceau, are the exquisite drapes and Austrian blinds of lightweight silk and the wall-to-wall carpet designed to harmonize with the wall covering. A fabric-covered ottoman in the center serves as a table and provides storage space.

The famous Jacques Grange style is displayed in its most perfect form in the living room. A Neo-Gothic screen provides a background for a sofa and a table by Emilio Terri. In front of the sofa, a table by Dunand is flanked by two Art Deco armchairs. On the far wall, in the library, are some of the designer's beloved photographs, which include portraits of Baudelaire, George Sand and Victor Hugo. On the mantelpiece (*above*) is a bust by Gimond; this corner of the room is simple in its arrangement and muted in color – but the windows look out on the green world of the Palais Royal gardens.

Left and below: An iron bedstead of delicately graphic silhouette sets the tone of this bedroom. Graphic too are the stripes of the wallpaper, the Neo-Gothic bench in front of the fireplace, and the arrangement of the pictures whose gold frames harmonize with the autumnal coloring of the room.

A guest bedroom, decorated as for the master of the chateau's daughter, is almost filled by a Louis XV canopied bedstead.

The centrally positioned library is the first room you enter in the apartment. Notice the contrasting character of the angular slate desk, the unusual chair, and the simple wooden bookshelves.

In the sitting room, a chintz patterned with lavish peonies in blue-and-white china vases sets off the paintings and 19th-century portraits, among them a large watercolor by Isabelle de Borchgrave above the console table. Two small, refined details, not be missed, are the ball of dried rosebuds on a curtain tieback, and the Chinese teapot that inspired the design of the fabric.

The entrance hall/library. The geometrical pattern of the carpet, the stripes of the Austrian blind, and the flowers on the walls harmonize with the golden oak woodwork.

Right: A genuine 18th-century color scheme sings out in the drawing room. Note the clever arrangement of drawings, prints, miniatures and ornaments on the walls, and the seating grouped to form several separate areas.

Candy shades – chiefly mint – color the bedroom, centered on a
great fourposter bed. Seashells and other little mementos are
enclosed in two glass tables.

Opposite: Birgitta Fouret's office perfectly indicates both her taste and her national origin. Note the Swedish chair in front of the roll-top desk, the pair of English children's armchairs upholstered in Paisley shawls, and the rare collection of objects made of Swedish Alvdalen porphyry on the mantelpiece. Here as elsewhere in the apartment the floor is stained black.

Above: In the study/library, seal impressions, cameos and medals are framed and hung against a background of red fabric – an inventive way of gathering small items together and displaying them to advantage.

In the living room, seats with simple white slipcovers partner
unusual pieces of Swedish 19th-century furniture. Points to note:
the casually positioned throws of antique striped silk, and the simple
Scandinavian style drapes of lightweight fabric at the windows.

Top: The bedroom is simple and light, but given spice by the pimento red hangings of the fourposter bed and the drapes. A kilim in the same tones is laid over wall-to-wall carpeting, and a bench is silhouetted against the window.

Above: The hall is made to seem longer by repetition of the decorative elements – kilims, Swedish chests of drawers, Karl Johan chairs covered with kilim, and a large collection of engravings from William Cavendish's 17th-century book on horsemanship.

A
WANDERING
SOUL

This sunny room on the top floor of a Parisian apartment building, stuffed with exotic treasures, looks rather like the home of Marco Polo, back from his long travels in the East. In fact it belongs to someone almost as romantic – an antique dealer turned historical novelist, Sylvie Simon. As a writer, she can bring to life heroines of the past such as Isabella d'Este and the Napoleonic Duchesse d'Abrantès; how alert she must be to the voices of her Chinese, Burmese and Japanese furniture, her Romantic and Pre-Raphaelite paintings, her Far Eastern objets d'art and sculptured busts! These objects crowding in from faraway places and faraway times stand out against the white walls of her apartment as the characters in a book stand out against its white pages. They constitute the decorative grammar of the place – not surprisingly, perhaps, in the home of a writer . . .

The apartment consists essentially of a single large room, from which a flight of steps leads up to a roof terrace. Among the many intriguing objects one might single out four 19th-century busts of colored marble representing the seasons, and a 19th-century Japanese mirror in its original tasseled frame.

Opposite: An 18th-century lacquer box from Burma stands on a Chinese lacquer chest of drawers of the same date. *Above:* Around the piano, itself of a glossy lacquer black, pictures tell tales from three centuries – the 18th, in a scene of a family in the country, the 19th, in an English oil of a galloping horse, and the 20th, in the large Japanese figure painting on panel. *Right:* A 19th-century Japanese ironwood chair.

METAMORPHOSIS IN THE MARAIS

Sic transit gloria domus – the glory of the house is passed away . . .
This palatial apartment on the main floor of one of the oldest houses
in the Marais was in a sorry state when the painter Gaston Berthelot
moved in a few years ago. The previous occupants had been a firm of
porcelain manufacturers, and the only surviving indications of past
grandeur were the proportions of the rooms themselves, and the stone
and parquet floors. To attempt a restoration of the original
appearance would have been not only expensive but dubious; and so
the artist called on his imagination to breathe life back into the
shell. On the walls, stripped of their paneling, he used sponged
paintwork in three colors taken from a fresco by Tiepolo; to furnish
the enfilade of three large rooms, no carpets, just a few pieces of
furniture, seats covered with white linen like the summer dust-covers
in an Italian palazzo; and to give a feeling of authenticity, antique
chandeliers hung in a traditional way. It is a style of decoration that
seems improvised, of the sort popular in the 17th century – and the
20th century too.

This vast room, originally an antechamber, now serves as a studio for
Gaston Berthelot, who prefers its warm southern light. The table, a Second
Empire copy of one by Cressent, holds paints and brushes grouped together
in pots.

The drawing room, illuminated in the afternoon by sun from the garden
and in the evening by candles – real and counterfeit – in candlesticks and
chandeliers. Note the textured effect of the walls, achieved with colored
glazes; the white linen draped casually over the seats; and the sleeves
covering the chandelier chains, which match the taffeta drapes.

Left: A view down the enfilade from the studio past the drawing room (formerly a picture gallery) to the bedroom, transformed into a sitting room.

Opposite: The end of the vista: a console table, placed in front of an antique mirror, displays an early 17th-century fountain of Rouen faience and a pair of ducks from Tunisia, where the painter often goes in search of inspiration.

The clean white kitchen (occupying the space of several utility rooms), with its collection of blue-and-white plates, has a Scandinavian look.

The living room, fitted into the attic by an ingenious architect. Notice the staircase, half concealed, that leads up to a bathroom tucked in at a slightly higher level, and the original attic window that illuminates a Louis XV writing table.

AFTER THE BALL

This room once echoed to waltzes and quadrilles: it was the ballroom of a private house, built out over the garden in the early years of this century. When the music stopped it became a storeroom, and then was forgotten. A young antique dealer with a particular love of unusual and out-of-the-way places recently set up home here, after doing the bare minimum of alterations in order to squeeze in a bedroom, kitchen and bathroom. He enlarged the original fountain and surrounded it with steps, and added two more columns to the original ones of granite. The effect is of a patio – in Granada, near the gardens of the Generalife? in the residential district of Beirut? No: in Paris, in the home of that most hospitable man, Maroun Salloum. With an array of guests – there is room for ten, or twenty, of fifty – you can dine beside the pool under the palm trees, listening to civilized conversation, and imagine yourself a thousand miles away. With a past like that, what does the future hold?

Previous pages
In the great room four potted palms around the pool stand on marble steps, which serve as seats at parties. On the walls at the back and behind the table by Diego Giacometti on the right are 18th-century prints depicting battles fought by the Emperor Chien Lung. In one corner a table covered with a 19th-century Indian carpet supports a pyramid of pomegranates in a 19th-century cooler, a Chinese vase, and a "maître d'hôtel cat" by Diego Giacometti, backed by a golden 17th-century Japanese screen.

The owner has an antique dealer's eye for mixing different periods and cultures.
Opposite: A 19th-century Austrian circular table and a Japanese table are seen against two strips of late 18th-century French Chinoiserie wallpaper. *Right:* The low table is a 19th-century English folding daybed; on it stands an 18th-century Imari pot. In the background are 19th-century crystal girandoles and 18th-century Italian craftsmen's masterworks.

EVERY OBJECT
TELLS A STORY

"A place for everything, and everything in its place:" that might be the ruling principle of this enlightened art-lover, surrounded by a profusion of diverse and remarkable objects from the past. He collects things for the simple pleasure of looking at them, but best of all he loves the ones that chime with the style of his apartment. He has a particular passion for unusual objects with intriguing histories, such as a chandelier whose miraculous escape from a fire is as

important to him as its shape. The fact that a picture frame was made for the Palais Rose in the great days of the dashing Count Boni de Castellane delights him at least as much as its carved and gilded swirls. What if there appears to be no story? Then he does research, even goes so far as to take something to pieces to understand its mysteries. Or, with a bit of trompe l'oeil *paintwork, he invents a past – and at a stroke a future – so that everything tells a story.*

The drawing room walls are covered with strawpaper painted in a shade of pink that enhances the paintings. The curtains of silk doupion are also pink, while the doors are grained, with black moldings. Over the fireplace is a 17th-century French painting between two 18th-century Meissen jars, while on either side Louis XV sconces, bronze plaques and framed panels are arranged symmetrically. Note the little picture on a low easel positioned like a fire guard.

Opposite: Again in the drawing room, symmetry extends to the placing of the two black leather chesterfields. A bust by Houdon, of terracotta finished to look like bronze, stands next to the door leading to the dining room. An English square piano is used as a table to display 16th- and 17th-century bronzes and a cabinetmaker's masterwork.

Right: The sitting room. Among the pictures hung against the 1930s wallpaper is a drawing in red chalk by Boucher.

Above: Delectable deception in the dining room: the table looks like terracotta, the walls seem to be covered with trellising, and you could almost swear the cornice was Wedgwood.

Opposite: In the bedroom, a big American brass bed faces the finest work in the room, Van Loo's *Experiment with Electricity*, above the fireplace.

The summer living room, in soft shades of ochre, almond green and pale blue, opens onto the terrace. The poetic mood of the house is summed up in the chaise longue – perfect for daydreaming – the birdcage and the baskets of flowers.

FANTASY ON A COUNTRY AIR

Falling in love or moving house can happen for the most unexpected reasons . . . "Two washhouses and five springs [on the estate] made me decide to buy the shell of the house. The garden is my passion and my inspiration, and I walk in it every day." These pastoral sentiments come from the well-known decorator Yves Taralon, a designer of fabrics and of major international exhibitions: though he is thoroughly Parisian, he now lives and works sixty kilometers from the capital. When he found it the house was a burned out ruin; he transformed it into an idyllic country retreat where poetry and comfort are perfectly balanced, full of inventive ideas, and rich with the spirit of France. Of course, he denies that any of this has been "designed." His professional skill comes through in the handling of volume and the management of space, but basically the house is an expression of the things he loves: friendship, good food, gaiety and simplicity – the things that matter in life.

Eye-catching simplicity: flowers and glass-chimneyed candlesticks on a stone ledge; garden chairs, tilted inward at the end of the day; and the white-shuttered house seen across the garden in spring.

Opposite: A corner of the terrace. You can almost smell the roses after rain.

Above: The laundries on the estate no longer echo to the bustle of washerwomen. This one has become a haven for the reader in search of quiet, the dreamer in search of solitude.

Special touches in the dining room include the slipcovering of
alternate chairs to give variety and the use of a starched white
tablecloth over a patterned one. On the table, basil plants in china
pots scent the air more deliciously than any potpourri.

Right: The relaxed atmosphere of the living room is created from a
host of imaginative details – wheat, green and growing, in an old
stone mortar next to the 1820s fireplace; a 19th-century *torchère* in
Pompeian style; the faded look of the paint on the walls, which
takes skill to achieve; the friendly old-fashioned armchairs freshly
slipcovered for summer; and the intriguing plaster tables, made by
John Dickinson in the late 1970s.

Opposite and below: Yves Taralon's bedroom is suffused with terracotta tones. The tan leather and chrome chair strikes a contemporary note, while the little cluster of things around the desk betrays the designer's pet interests – objects from Japan, photographs of the Palais de Chaillot in Paris, and flowers from the garden.

Right: In the study, hung with fabric from Alsace, there are large mahogany bookcases and a vast desk of light-colored wood. The lamp, here as elsewhere, is made from an antique candlestick.

HARMONICS

Henri Garelli, known as a maestro of design, likes to think in musical terms. His golden rule is, "In every interior design scheme there must be, as it were, a harmonic progression." In this Palladian villa he has orchestrated styles and colors like a musician composing a symphony. Starting with the reception rooms, marked "allegro con fuoco," and passing on to the bedrooms, to be played "andante," the movements succeed one another and lead up to the "finale con brio" – a lavish swimming pool. This decorative score is written in a major key and played without a single false note, leaving the audience relaxed and delighted.

In a composition conceived by the landscapist Alain Fey (*below*) a checkerboard of stone and grass leads the eye back to a teak bench framed by timber uprights and a swing. The garden in front of the pedimented house (*right*) is worthy of Vuillard.

One whole wall of the library/smoking room is lined with a 19th-century glass-fronted bookcase. The Paisley pattern upholstery fabric echoes the colors of the Savonnerie carpet.

The bathroom is typical of Henri Garelli's refined mastery of the mixing of genres. A 19th-century copper bathtub is set into an alcove, below an English glazed triptych. A Restauration petit-point carpet and stool, and a Napoleon III shaving stand of silvered metal, complete the effect of old-fashioned charm.

Tea in the garden, in a delightful summerhouse of stripped wood that the designer found in another garden. In this bower, already beginning to be covered with roses, the atmosphere is of an idyllic past, evoking the novels of E. M. Forster or Edith Wharton.

A sitting room is arranged as a winter garden, around an original fountain that is still in working order. *Opposite:* The symmetrical columns suggested the choice and placing of the furniture, which includes a daybed, Napoleon III chairs with buttoned upholstery, and a Louis XIV console table. *Right:* The same room, seen from the entrance hall. The only concession to modern taste is the use of wicker cachepots.

THE HOUSE OF FLOWERS

Some country houses are so elegant that they look like apartments in town. Others are so rustic that they look like parodies of country inns. This one takes its cue, appropriately enough, from the surrounding garden, and effortlessly succeeds in being what a real country house should be. It has white shutters, a covering of Virginia creeper, a smooth lawn and a few fruit trees, and above all a profusion of flowers – in flowerbeds, compositions, bouquets, drawings, printed fabrics and papers – both out-of-doors and in every room. For Patrick Lavoix, the owner, who is a fashion designer for Lanvin Hommes, is obsessed with flowers. He photographs them, season by season, to record their colors, and he has made them the decorative theme of his house. In the bedrooms they appear, unobtrusively, in the fabrics of the beds, drapes, and armchairs. In the dining room you will find them on the chairs – and blossoming on the chandelier. In the salon they bloom in profusion on seats and lampshades, screens and ottomans, window blinds and tables, and, as in the garden, their colors and shapes intermingle with a freedom that is utterly natural.

Above: At one end of the house, an awning like those used in Italian markets creates a shady terrace on the lawn.

Opposite: Lunch under a cherry tree, outside the vine-clad house. Light folding chairs have been repainted to match the white iron table.

The art of indoor gardening: there are more than fifteen different kinds of flower in the living room, but the dazzling mixture of colors is offset by the rough stone of the walls and the soft green of the carpet. Two ideas to remember are the books tucked in above the window on the right, and the low table made up of an iron balcony and a sheet of plate glass.

The sitting room with a
19th-century flavor is
organized around a
fireplace topped with a
plain sheet of mirror
glass. Gouaches of
Naples hang above the
Empire sofa. The
marble floor is covered
with rush matting. The
low table is made up of
a mahogany column
drum and a granite
slab. A group of 1930s
stoneware vases gleam
under the light beside
the fireplace, while on
the mantel stand
faience figurines from
Dinan in Brittany.

BETWEEN WIND AND TIDE

This island in the Atlantic with its temperate climate, its unique light and its wonderful ever-changing sky has its devotees, fanatics who would not trade its salty landscape for all the palm trees in the world. Some thirty years ago, a Parisian fell head over heels in love with the place, and bought some old abandoned buildings that had formerly been used by oyster farmers. Where there had been nothing but drained marshland she created a garden, and restored the five little houses to make a magical holiday refuge for her children and grandchildren. Each room, filled with country furniture and family possessions, is a snug haven – but every window gives a glimpse of the nearby sea and the long rows of oyster beds left exposed as the tide creeps out.

Above: A vestibule between living room and bedrooms. On the left is a fall-front desk made on the island in the 18th century; on the right, a dresser from the area, transformed to hold a collection of books about the sea.

Opposite: A corner of the living room, with its open timber roof. The walls are of thinly plastered stone, the floor of waxed brick. The 18th-century stone mantelpiece was discovered on the island, in a shepherd's hut.

In the spaces that now form the living room wines and spirits were stored and oysters were collected for shipping. Old sea-chests and a loom are reminders of the lives of local fishermen and their wives in bygone days. A glass-fronted *bonnetière* in the background (*left*) displays local faience. In one corner of the room (*above*) an old well was retained: it is twenty meters from the sea, and fills with salt water every time the tide comes in.

A stone-paved path extends from the living room out into the garden, and also gives access to three separate little guest houses.

Above: A large canvas by Yves Lévêque entitled *The Hen* broods over the living room. The decorative objects include antique balls for the bowling game of *pétanque*, and a weathervane propped up casually in a corner.

Opposite: In the entrance hall, as golden as a harvest field, the visitor is greeted by an 18th-century *tribulum*, a rasp-like board drawn by horses to thresh grain.

A MEDIEVAL CHATEAU BROUGHT BACK TO LIFE

Is it possible to restore youth and beauty to a chateau of which the oldest parts go back to the Middle Ages and the youngest to the 18th century? The present owners fell in love with the building, and determined to do just that. It took years of work and patience, but the result was a triumphant success – a success due to their perfectionism and taste. Perfectionism, as they ensured that when any materials had to be replaced, such as beams, flooring or woodwork, the replacements were either authentic features salvaged from elsewhere or faithful reproductions made by local craftsmen, and that traditional techniques were used in their installation. Taste, as they created a particularly subtle mixture of old and new that delights the eye and enhances the quality of life, antique provincial furniture blending happily with cool modernity to produce a truly lived-in feel. The result of this conjugation of past and present? Pluperfect.

Opposite: Turrets with "Genoese" roofs cling to the corners of the house. The austerity of the walls is offset by the shutters, painted a gray-blue that is distinctive to the area.

Right: Loose hangings of heavy ecru linen soften the exposed stonework of the entrance hall.

The spacious, simple, country kitchen. The terracotta floor tiles, restored open timber ceiling, and rustic bench give it a traditional air. A sophisticated note is struck by the Dutch brass chandelier, its gleam echoed in the row of copper pans.

Opposite: The bedroom of the mistress of the house has an 18th-century flavor, with its mantelpiece of painted wood, overmantel, mirror, screen and fruitwood secretaire. The Cogolin carpet is modern.

Right: A happy marriage of old and new. A Louis XVI bed and an antique chair from Southern France are matched with a modern painting by Jean-Louis Germain.

ATMOSPHERE . . .

Are we in 1870 or a hundred years later? Is this one of those interiors lovingly recorded by painters in the second half of the 19th century, or the modern home of people with a flair for comfort and style? The near-perfection of Jean-Louis Riccardi's designs makes the question almost impossible to answer. Here at La Grave Bechade, a chateau in the Bordeaux region, Riccardi used all his imagination to recreate the muffled, exquisite atmosphere of a bygone age. But his choice of fabrics, the way he mixes printed patterns, and his placing of furniture are lessons for any genre.

The use of two main colors, darkish red and sky blue, gives the living room a distinctive air, while the unusual combination of different prints based on roses and broad stripes, for curtains, walls, carpet and upholstery, pushes distinction to the point of daring. Balancing this profusion is the symmetrical placing of twin lamps, sofas, armchairs and corner cupboards.

Blue and red appear again in the dining room — blue for the wall coverings and curtains of printed moire and the velvet of the chairs, red for the bergère. Both colors tone in with the mahogany furniture, the walnut paneling, and the patterned carpet by Jean-Louis Riccardi. In his choice of objects, the designer gave free reign to that feeling that drives us to hunt around in junk shops for exciting finds: the table is Louis XVI, the chairs are 19th-century and American, the brass chandelier is of the 1880s, and the terracotta statues, raised to the right height on simple cubic bases, date from the 18th century.

PASSION'S FRUITS

To come upon this hidden place is a magical experience. Imagine, at the end of a garden of studied naturalness, an elegantly simple house. There is an Italianate quality to its façade that speaks of the South. Within, you are in the domain of a man of culture and humor, the favorite retreat of a painter in love with color and flowers. In this house with a long history, built in the reigns of Louis XIII, Louis XIV and Louis XV and then partly restored in the 19th century (as was so often done in the cause of "progress"), the furniture too comes from different periods, and feels like a family collection acquired over the centuries. It sets the tone, but remains in the background: for here objects rule. Objects of all kinds! *Animalier* bronzes, terracotta putti, cups made of agate and other semiprecious stones, prints, drawings, skilfully framed sketches in red chalk, curiously shaped boxes, unusual candlesticks, grouped into spontaneous compositions by the hand of an artist, ornament the rooms. Potted plants proliferate. There are tapestry-covered cushions by the dozen. But the style of living cultivated by the master of this house is unique; and the warmth of his welcome a rare thing.

The present façade and the cast-iron balustrade date from the 19th century, but the stairs with their double flight were built in the early 18th century on early 17th-century foundations.

Opposite: In the living room on the ground floor three new round-headed arches were created, echoing the form of the windows, so that daylight now comes in from both sides. The space beyond the arches is like an orangery, sheltering plants in the winter.

FROM ANOTHER CENTURY

The second half of the 19th century was an age of comfort and profusion, when private life was raised to the level of art. Its style of interior decoration was long despised in favor of severer forms, but now its decoration and architecture are fashionable again. One of its most passionate supporters is the designer Robert d'Ario. Among his works is this house in Toulouse, where he used fabrics and carpets specially copied from historic models, and indulged his love of antiques and authentic period detail. Behind these dazzling wonders lies every convenience that the late 20th century could desire.

The house (*above*) is classical in form, and its doors and windows are surrounded, in Toulouse fashion, with bricks as rosy as the tiles of the roof. Not far away is a pergola (*right*), arranged like a conservatory with plants in large terracotta pots and climbing shrubs. The curly cane furniture and carpet are modern. The fine wooden screens have the delightful effect of a veil through which one glimpses a lush green world.

Two strong details that sum up the style of the house and Robert d'Ario's love of Second Empire modes of decoration. *Opposite:* The use of the same fabric wallcovering in the entrance hall and the informal sitting room creates a layered effect. The curly pediment over the door is contemporary with the Neo-Gothic chair. *Right:* The same pattern continues up the stairs and covers a little chair on the landing. The wall surface is further enriched by a collection of 19th-century German watercolors, extended to an infinite vista in the mirror.

Left: Inside the veranda – an exotic world of tropical plants and Asian bamboo furniture.

Below: The Taris' favorite corner of the garden, beside an artificial lake surrounded by ancient trees.

The kitchen is a
delicious mixture of
different ingredients.
The chairs in early
16th-century style and
the early 20th-century
chandelier might almost
be amusing finds from
a junk shop; the wall
tiles were made at Apt
in Provence; and the
idea of masonry niches
for storage is Mexican.

A bedroom in the chateau, updated to the 1980s. A miller's ladder leads to the clothes closet on the upper level; beyond is an ultra-modern bathroom.

An eclectic interior with a wonderful sense of unity. Scarcely any two things in this little family living room are of the same date or origin. There are low Napoleon III chairs covered with tapestry and a Régence bergère upholstered in a plain pale fabric; a 19th-century painted tin tray on an English mahogany folding support and a modern table made of wood and glass; an Orientalist painting over the fireplace and a collection of 1930s objects; and on the floor a patchwork of rugs from different regions of the Middle East.

The real living room at
Giscours is the library
with its surrounding
gallery. The shelves, of
elm, contain not only
books but a special
section of international
magazines, and polo
photographs and prizes.
There are hunting
trophies from far-off
lands, and, as elsewhere
in the house, a richly
eclectic blend of
furniture and objects.

ONTHEFRINGEOFTHE 19th CENTURY

Two designers from Bordeaux, Jean-François Braconnier and Christophe Larquey, applied all their skill to restore a mansion in the old quarter of Bordeaux to the appearance it might have had in the later 19th century, with antique furniture and objets d'art placed in an authentic setting. A brilliant stylistic exercise, this: chairs with buttoned upholstery, fabrics trimmed with fringe and braid, little occasional tables, patterned carpets, paintings, stained glass, rubber plants – not a tassel or a leaf is missing. In the ornately decorated suite of three rooms that forms the heart of the house, we wander – amazed, intrigued, and delighted – in the great age of bourgeois opulence.

The central space, which is living room, bedroom and library all in one, has the snug atmosphere of a 19th-century smoking room. Key elements are the antique carpet of embroidered felt, the comfortable fireside chair covered with old fabric, the fringed ottoman, the 1870s Minton vase poised on a wooden column, and the portrait (by Jacques Leman) of a man whom we might well take for the master of the house.

Opposite: The salon, a classical 18th-century-style room such as you find in all Second Empire interiors. The ornate gilt furniture is Italian, of the third quarter of the 19th century.

The living room/bedroom/library is separated from the winter garden by blue drapes, which herald the shift from warm artificial light to cool daylight. The 1830s Austrian bed, the Biedermeier chair drawn up to a writing table suitably covered with baize, the Minton majolica vases, the folding screen decorated with landscape scenes, and even the elaborate moldings of the ceiling all conspire to create the sort of interior that was fashionable in the late 19th century not only in France but in Central Europe and England as well.

The 19th century had a special passion for winter gardens. This one was devised around a stained glass panel by the famous glass-painter Caranze. Points to note: the matching pair of upholstered armchairs, authentic right down to their elaborate fringe and tassels, the divan with its cording and braid, and the modern carpet with a 19th-century flavor to its stripes, by Madeleine Castaing. Something to remember is how the green of the potted plants adds intensity to the turquoise tones that are used in the room.

In the living room, the visitor is greeted by a portrait of the mistress of the house, painted by the master (*left*). Early pieces of furniture in dark wood and 19th-century sofas covered with stamped velvet play a discreet supporting role to Bernard Buffet's paintings. An 18th-century bronze of the infant Hercules stands on the marble table in the foreground. Elsewhere in the living room (*below left*), a painting by Buffet of a church hangs above a medieval statue of the Virgin in polychromed wood; on either side are bronze figures of animals by Rosa and Isidore Bonheur.

Opposite: A 19th-century circular mahogany table gives another glimpse of the collections that enliven the house, among them an Empire statuette, cloisonné enamel vases, and tortoise shells.

The kitchen/dining room, approached from a little sitting room with white slipcovered chairs (*opposite*), offers an appetizing mixture of simplicity and sophistication. The 19th-century mahogany furniture is English. On the walls, above the tiling, are plates with the arms of the city of Nancy, made by Gallé, and antique pots of Moustiers faience. A recess serves to display 18th-century French and English silver. The gilt bronze and opaline hanging lamp introduces an ornate note of luxury.

FOR LOVE OF THE VINE

The Lubéron is known as a cultivated region. Writers, directors, musicians and intellectuals in all fields choose to come here in their moments of freedom. And what is actually cultivated there? Fruit, lavender, and the occasional grapevine. The most recently established vineyard is that of Val Joannis: the estate, created a few years ago by a wealthy buinessman, includes a handsome bastide which was restored and decorated by his wife. Their house, like their wine, has the qualities that age well.

A wrought-iron gate leads into the courtyard of the house, which is paved with river pebbles like the old threshing-floors in the region. The table is laid in the shade of an immense *micocoulier* or African lotus tree, a Provençal relative of the elm.

A SILK FARM TRANSFORMED

Like several other houses in this part of Provence, this 17th-century complex was originally a silk farm. The designer Françoise de Pfyffer transformed it into a holiday house, adding to its comfort without diminishing its character, making it more modern but scarcely less authentic in feeling. The rooms used to house the silkworms became the drawing room, dining room and kitchen, the attics became bedrooms, and the big lean-to sheltering the well became a vast gallery/

living room linking what had originally been two separate buildings. The furnishings are sober. A few dark pieces of country furniture, local pottery and glass, and the use on beams and shutters of a blue like that of the copper sulfate dusted on the nearby vineyards — so much for the region. A few bold modern works of art, a few handsome antiques — so much for decoration from elsewhere. Under the matchless light of Provence, the two worlds live very comfortably together.

Holidays, happiness, sun and the South . . . From a window, the view is like a Cézanne. Below is a terrace, covered with gravel in the Mediterranean way, with a table sheltered by a wisteria-clad pergola.

The gallery/living room, lit by an immense window, houses the old well, on which stand a bouquet in the colors of sunshine and a sculpture by Arman. The chaise longue is 18th-century, as is the carved lion. The Greek carpet is modern.

An entrance hall, at one end of the building. The ceiling, with its alternation of exposed beams and plaster, is typical of old houses in Provence. The straw hats on the table come from every quarter of the globe.

The gallery. The ceiling beams are painted yellow and the walls are whitewashed; the floor is paved with stone from Ménerbes. Set against this simplicity are a large canvas by Philippe Leroy and an ancestor portrait, a piano with a stool by Diego Giacometti and (looking at a glance like a tray of drinks) a paper sculpture by Pavlos.

Top: In a bedroom, dazzling white was chosen for the painted floor, the plain linen curtains, the bedspread of Provençal cotton lace and the stone bedside tables.

Above: The dining room table is lit by an antique hanging lamp from a store. The dishes on the right-hand wall are antique tin-glazed earthenware from Apt (see also p. 211). The drapes and the squab cushions on the chairs are made of blue-and-white-striped mattress ticking.

Right: A cozy drawing room, designed with autumn days in mind. Note the low table by Diego Giacometti, the sculpture by Christo on the mantelpiece, and, on the walls, a work by César and a drawing by Paul Rotterdam.

METAMORPHOSIS AT MOUGINS

When it was discovered by Patrick and Jo Frémontier, two antique dealers from Cannes, this house at Mougins was like countless others – a low pink-washed rectangle, vaguely Provençal in flavor, with a fine view of the sea. Now, heightened by one story, broadened by two wings, pierced with large windows, accented by dark lines, rejuvenated, one might even say styled, it is definitely one-of-a-kind. If you look very hard you might discern an influence from Rome, something of Scandinavia, even perhaps a whiff of California.

Certainly it provides every pleasure imaginable in a handsome, sophisticated, Mediterranean house.

The façade covered with dark green trellising looks as though it had been drawn with a pen. The story added above the roof terrace contains an extra bedroom.

Top: A living room entering the garden, or how to use a modern bay window. The opulent cushioned stools came from an old mansion on the Riviera.

Above: A spot for a siesta, under an awning by the swimming pool. Note the lawn, where a pattern is formed from squares of grass and slabs of stone, and the panels of trellis work that symbolically shelter the pool from the house.

Above: The walls of the living room, painted stone color, enclose a collection of objects of diverse provenance – Etruscan vases on the mantelpiece, an inlaid marble table top which began life as part of a floor in a palace in Naples, Roman antiquities, and a 17th-century allegorical painting of Hercules.

Opposite: The entrance door is flanked by columns bearing Neo-Classical urns. On the table is a curious commemorative model from America.

ACKNOWLEDGMENTS

This book could never have been realized without the very generous cooperation of the owners who allowed us into their houses and apartments: to them I extend my warmest thanks. My gratitude goes too to the *Maison & Jardin* team, and in particular to Christine Grange-Bary, Lisa Roussel, Françoise de Valence and Aude de La Conté. Finally I am also indebted, for their help, to Jean-Marie Baron, Nanou Billault, Marie-Claire Blanckaert, Sonia Dieudonné, Jean-Louis Gaillemin, Marie-Jo de Loisne, Claudine Mulard and Florence Trocmé.

Daphné de Saint Sauveur

From darkness to dazzling light, in the secret garden of an old farm in Provence.

REFERENCES AND CREDITS

The picture stories from which the present book has been designed appeared originally in *Maison & Jardin*. The list that follows gives the title of each article, the date of publication, and the name of the photographer.

p.1
"Les dimanches de Victor Laloux"
February 1987
Jacques Bachmann

p.2
"Le XIXᵉ en toute intimité"
February 1987
Jacques Bachmann

p.6
"Les dimanches de Victor Laloux"
see above, p.1

p.11
"70 m² de candeur et de naturel"
see below, pp. 28–31

pp.12–17
"Les feux de l'automne"
October 1987
Roland Beaufre

pp.18–21
"Le petit théâtre de la vie"
October 1987
Roland Beaufre

pp.22–7
"Un réveil en beauté"
October 1987
Pascal Chevallier

pp.28–31
"70 m² de candeur et de naturel"
October 1986
Jacques Bachmann

pp.32–7
"Chez une jeune femme rangée"
April 1987
Roland Beaufre

pp.38–41
"Un passé très présent"
September 1985
Jacques Primois

pp.42–7
"Le style Plaine Monceau"
December 1985/January 1986
Pascal Hinous

pp.48–55
"A Jacques Grange, lettre de château"
October 1985
François Halard

p.57
"Le goût du bien-être"
February 1986
Pascal Chevallier

pp.58–63
"Couleur de bonheur"
February 1988
Pascal Chevallier

pp.64–9
"Le show des choses"
March 1987
Roland Beaufre

pp.70–73
"L'âme voyageuse: un avant-goût de romanesque"
September 1987
Roland Beaufre